'Western Values Defended' by Olivia Pierson is an eloquent reminder that superstition is the enemy of enlightenment. It is a series of salutary snapshots from the last two millennia illustrating the pitched battle the forces of reason and its corollaries, freedom and prosperity, have had to wage against unreason and *its* corollaries, deprivation and barbarism. It is tempting, in our current context, to believe that Islam is the sole repository of the latter; Pierson's primer, while justly indicting Islam, is also a sobering testament that in its heyday, Christianity could be just as virulent—and that, to paraphrase and juxtapose one of the book's icons, Thomas Jefferson, the price of liberty is eternal hostility to *any* form of tyranny over the minds of men. Fashionable multiculturalism, she points out also, is one such form. 'Western Values Defended,' by contrast, is a proud paean to each human individual's inalienable rights to life, liberty and the pursuit of happiness.

— Lindsay Perigo, Broadcaster, Editor, Author, Commentator, Speech & Media coach

"Know your history boy," an old Irishman once advised me. And yet how many really do know the history of the civilisation they take so much for granted, and so many so openly despise. Olivia Pierson has written a short, sharp, easily-read primer for anyone who does want to know this glorious history—and why it was so glorious. You might argue that it's no sin not to know your history. But it is when it's made this easy to discover — and who knows? You may even discover it wasn't all made by dead white males.

— P⸻ ⸻ecture & Own⸻

Western Values Defended
A Primer

Olivia Pierson

ISBN-13: 978-0-473-35435-0
ISBN-10: 0-473-35435-7

Cover Art – Raphael's School of Athens

Printed in the United States of America

This book is dedicated to my high-spirited ancestors, to my beloved children, Shandra, Zach and Ruby, and to their yet unborn children.

> *The lips of time leech to the fountain head;*
> *Love drips and gathers, but the fallen blood*
> *Shall calm her sores.*
> *And I am dumb to tell a weather's wind*
> *How time has ticked a heaven round the stars.*

> *"The Force That Through The Green Fuse Drives The Flower"*
> *by Dylan Thomas*

CONTENTS

INTRODUCTION

You may think it a strange thing to be writing about defending Western values in a Western country in the year 2016. One of the benefits of being alive during the latter half of the 20th Century and the early decades of the 21st is that we in the free democratic world have enjoyed an unprecedented time of peace, made possible by the victory of two vicious World Wars, fought by our forefathers, the result being the spectacular triumph of the cause of liberty over tyranny.

We, the children and grandchildren of those brave forefathers, have never been exposed to life without our individual liberties intact. They throb in the very heart of our civilization, defining its daily character. But we have never had to rise to defend them in any meaningful sense because we have not had them threatened, as those who came before us did.

Make no mistake: our liberties are not given to us as a matter of permanent inheritance. It is up to each generation to protect them as the values they are in fact. What we fail to actively value, we fail to actively protect. When we fail to protect things that are precious, they get stolen, or lost, or smashed.

All Westerners love their freedom and cannot imagine life on any other terms. When I ask the average person what our civilization's defining values are, they don't have an answer but can only repair to generalizations such as freedom, or liberty. They seldom can identify what the best of our values are. The aim of this small book is to correct that.

THE AGE OF REASON

During the 18th Century something truly revolutionary started to happen in the minds of American and European people.

Since the total collapse of the great Roman Empire in the 7th Century AD, religion became the world's ruling power — Islam in the East, Catholicism in the West. These powers were known as "theocracies" from the Greek words: theo- meaning "god" and cracy- meaning "to rule". Religion was politics, and politics was religion.

The idea of a free thinking, free acting way of life was alien to this long epoch. Life was about submitting yourself to religious authority, and there were always plenty of popes, cardinals, archbishops, bishops, abbots, Jesuits, monks, deacons and priests overseeing communities to make sure that you did. Private conscience had very little to do with anything. Before 1538, as unbelievable as this sounds, it was illegal even to own an English bible (Latin was the only language deemed fit for the Lord's holy Word, and of course only those great bastions of holiness, ordained priests, could be relied upon for its accurate revelation). In 1525, Englishman William Tyndale translated the New Testament from its original Greek and Hebrew texts into English and then was legally strangled and burned at the stake for his troubles. They were not remembered as the Dark Ages for nothing.

The 18th Century men and women of the Age of Reason put an end to this long-standing tyranny in the Western world by a triumph of the human intellect.

The Scientific Revolution

Throughout the Middle Ages, the church had always maintained as a matter of Christian doctrine that the heavens; the stars, planets, moon and sun revolved around the earth because Earth was where God had created man — and man was the very pinnacle of his creation. But Nicolaus Copernicus in Prussia (1473), Galileo Galilei in Italy (1564) and Johannes Kepler in Germany (1571) discovered, through observations and mathematics, that it was the sun — the source of light — which was at the center of our solar system, not the earth. These men battled the religious powers of their day for these unpopular assertions, but out of these three it was only Galileo, perhaps because he lived in the very center of Catholic rule in Italy, who was successfully persecuted for his science. He was repeatedly summoned before the Roman Inquisition, the highest religious court of his time, to give account for his heretical teachings and writings.

Unlike his countryman, Giordano Bruno, who had also been tortured and burned alive by the Inquisition for heresy (his views on metaphysics and cosmology), Galileo was allowed to keep his life, but was held under house arrest and closely monitored for the last nine years of his existence. His most beloved, but illegitimate daughter, Virginia, died young and alone in a cold convent without the comfort of her father's love because he was forbidden by law to visit her. No, they were not remembered as the Dark Ages for nothing.

It was Isaac Newton in England (1642) who boldly advanced the Scientific Revolution through his formulation of the universal law of gravity, and his experiments on optics and the composition of light. Rather than being persecuted for his science, Newton was celebrated. The French philosopher and satirist Voltaire attended Newton's grand funeral in 1727 at Westminster Abbey. By this time the intellectual atmosphere in England had changed because they were no longer under Catholic rule. Science had accepted that the earth was not the center of the universe. Voltaire observed that Newton lived a long and relatively happy life in an age of liberty where scholarly inquiry was free:

"Reason alone was cultivated, and mankind could only be his [Newton's] pupil, not his enemy."

"His countrymen honored him in his lifetime, and interred him as though he had been a king who had made his people happy."

— *Letters on the English, Voltaire*

The Enlightenment

The Enlightenment can be thought of as a time when the mental lights of the common man started to glow brighter.

Newton's famous experiment in light, with a glass prism and a dark room showing how one single ray of light actually contained every single color in the spectrum unobservable to the naked eye, allowed any 18th Century person to demonstrate the same experiment to any group of people. A glass prism was a child's toy. Scientific experiments became an obsession with all classes of society — rich and poor. With the widespread use of the printing press fueling the availability of books, any person who could read could also educate themselves in matters of scientific discovery. Knowledge became a quest.

In England, natural philosophers — scientists — of this time were held in high public regard instead of persecuted. People looked less and less toward the Church for answers on how the world was in fact. Religion found itself in an ideological war with Reason. Reason won. The Enlightenment was a clap of intellectual thunder which rumbled around the European world for a hundred years, causing people to think and act differently.

During Newton's lifetime, the Protestant Reformation changed the very political structures of England. The King was now subject to a constitution and a parliament, making the style of government officially a Constitutional Monarchy. Catholics were not allowed to hold positions of governance. In fact, they were not even allowed to vote. By the time that George III took the throne in 1761, England owned significant colonies in North America & Canada, all loyal to the British Crown. America's Founding Fathers were to radically alter that.

Individual Rights

"When in the course of human events, it becomes necessary for one people to dissolve the political bands which have connected them with another, and to assume among the powers of the earth, the separate and equal station to which the Laws of Nature and of Nature's God entitle them, a decent respect to the opinions of mankind requires that they should declare the

causes which impel them to the separation."

Thus begins America's Declaration of Independence, authored by Thomas Jefferson; Virginian gentleman-farmer & slaveholder. He and his brothers-in-ideas have just informed King George III of England that the thirteen independent States in America no longer owe him any loyalty or allegiance. He has also made clear that they are happy to explain themselves and their actions, indeed, are bound by decency to do so.

"We hold these truths to be self evident, that all men are created equal, that they are endowed by their Creator with certain unalienable rights, that among these are Life, Liberty and the Pursuit of Happiness. That to secure these rights, Governments are instituted among Men, deriving their just powers from the consent of the governed. That whenever any form of Government becomes destructive of these ends, it is the Right of the People to alter or to abolish it, and to institute new Government, laying its foundation on such principles and organizing its powers in such form, as to them shall seem most likely to effect their Safety and Happiness."

Jefferson presumes to lecture George III on just what governments are invented for, the securing of individual rights. He goes on to fully endorse the right of citizens to throw off a government if it acts destructively toward its people.

"Prudence, indeed, will dictate that Governments long

established should not be changed for light and transient causes; and accordingly all experience hath shown, that mankind are more disposed to suffer, while evils are sufferable, than to right themselves by abolishing the forms to which they are accustomed. But when a long train of abuses and usurpations, pursuing invariably the same Object evinces a design to reduce them under absolute Despotism, it is their right, it is their duty, to throw off such Government, and to provide new Guards for their future security."

Jefferson states that they are aware that traditional political bonds of connection ought not to be thrown off lightly, but that history has shown people are more likely to put up with abuses and suffering, rather than extend the effort of abolishing the very governments which cause them. He reminds George III that it is not just a right of the people, but their *duty*, to secure a new and faithful government for themselves when a history of abuse has become the pattern.

Jefferson articulated Enlightenment thinking at its height. He spelled out clearly to George III that America considered him *unworthy to be the head of a free people*.

This wrote the end of America's once immovable loyalty to their beloved old empire. It was clear-cut treason.

This important document ignited a bloody six-year war with England, but America was to win its independence and has held it sacred ever since. They created a Constitutional Republic, with no king — that is, a country of laws to which every man and woman was subject, including the President and his whole administration.

Jefferson died in 1826 when Abraham Lincoln was an unknown seventeen year-old country woodcutter somewhere in Indiana. Armed with the thinking and political creations of The Enlightenment, he would go on to become one of America's most formidable presidents, the one who *authored* America's black population from slavery into freedom. The Emancipation Proclamation was to become the Constitution's 13th Amendment in 1865. Its effect was to bring the whole of America under one constitutional law as one nation of free individuals, but still with the freedom of broad interpretations of the law by each separate State — within Reason.

Apart from the Emancipation Proclamation, Lincoln's great achievement was to unite North & South. I can think of no other time anywhere in history where, during such a fierce and divisive war as the American Civil war proved to be, in its dark and gloomy midst the country still held a genuinely fair and free election, which voted Lincoln in for a second term. Almost every single family in the country lost at least a son to that war, yet a democratic election took place as a matter of national identity. That was the power and unifying virtue of being created a Constitutional Republic.

RELIGIOUS TOLERANCE

The most supreme gift to the modern world from
The Age of Reason was the legal divorce of religion &
state. It was an advanced and long overdue
acknowledgement that religion was a common cause
of unmatched strife between human beings, therefore
a hindrance to the progress of a peaceful civilization.
Man's recorded history is about 8000 - 10,000 years
old, while secular democratic governments are only
about 200. It is sometimes easy to forget that in the
affairs of humankind this legal separation is quite a
recent development.

In classical antiquity, under the Golden Age of
Athens (399 BCE) where a fledgling democracy was
in early bloom, Socrates was unusually put to death
for not believing in the correct gods. It was given to
a public vote where the philosophically-minded men
of Athens decided that quarrelsome old Socrates was
a detrimental influence on their young. Instead of
fleeing the city as any condemned person might have
done, he stayed and drank the fatal hemlock (perhaps
believing that Reason was a cause worth being

martyred for). The people of the city he loved had spoken. Some 77 years later Aristotle would meet with a similar verdict for a similar reason, but flee the city he did, saying, *"I will not allow the Athenians to sin twice against philosophy."*

After Alexander the Great conquered the known world (323 BCE), leaving Hellenistic culture in his wake, religious tolerance became something close to normal. (That may have had something to do with his being privately tutored by the liberal-minded Aristotle.)

The later Roman Republic also allowed for individual conscience to flourish, until the depravity of the Caesars, Caligula and Nero, started a horrific decline into the heavy persecution of Christians — and any others who believed their God was more worthy of worship than their Caesar. Eventually, after Emperor Constantine forcefully campaigned to end the persecution of Christians (330 AD), they gained ascendancy as the state religion of Rome to go on to become the steady persecutors of all other faiths, including different strains of their own.

Throughout the darkest age of medieval Europe where theocracy firmly held sway, religious tolerance was an irrelevant notion. Religion reigned supreme with Catholicism in the West and Islam in the East — any contradictions to the self-proclaimed wisdom of these monotheistic super-powers were swiftly met with persecution, torture and agonizing deaths. In the 16th Century, during the Protestant Reformation, which, against Catholic tyranny, asserted that liberty of conscience was a fundamentally biblical precept, it is estimated that over 12 million people lost their lives — and that is just in the West. Untold millions were put to the sword under Ottoman conquests, a difference in religious practice being the — pardon the expression — sticking point.

It would take another 200 years, a whole New World and some very committed Founding Fathers before the official separation of religion and state would become fully institutionalized as law. They knew that the only way to have peace preside over so many different religions was to have a state that remained religiously neutral. Freedom of religion also meant freedom *from* religion. The result was an America founded on the virtue of religious tolerance (and free speech). It is enshrined in the Constitution's First Amendment:

"Congress shall make no law respecting an establishment of religion, or prohibiting the free exercise thereof; or abridging the freedom of speech, or of the press; or the right of the people peaceably to assemble, and to petition the Government for a redress of grievances."

Yet even this enlightened measure did not eliminate

atrocities — the Mormons were expelled from Missouri in 1838, and Haun's Mill became the ominous landmark for a bloody massacre. Joseph Smith, Mormonism's founder, was not only subjected to being tarred and feathered by an angry religious mob, he was finally murdered within a jailhouse in Illinois. Catholics and Protestants suffered under each other's biases in American life early in the 19th Century, but nothing close to the scale of religious persecutions which had ravaged European lands, and continued to ravage the Ottoman Empire. These events underscored the point of the Founding Fathers' efforts, and the sense of urgency they had felt when setting religious tolerance in the stone of federal law.

Today almost all democratic governments have a version of the First Amendment, including Israel, India, East Timor and the Philippines. But conspicuously missing this essential civilizational gem are the Islamic countries, along with the underdeveloped countries with authoritarian regimes like Congo, North Korea and Haiti. China too, although developed, and with strong trading ties to the West, still cannot shake off its authoritarian super-ego, showing little regard for religious tolerance within its own borders.

Complete separation of religion and state is a government's concrete way of displaying respect for the free minds and individuality of its citizens. In the modern world where the path toward globalization is now well paved, we ought to hold some measure of rational suspicion in our dealings with other nation states if they have not yet afforded this fundamental decency to their own people. It shows a startling lack of esteem for human development, to say nothing of natural rights.

Hypatia of Alexandria: The Beautiful Lady in the Middle

When Raphael painted his famous classical work, School of Athens, he rendered the form of a beseeching figure in white robes who was the only female in the fresco. She is also the only philosopher steadily gazing straight out of the work to make eye contact with the viewer. Her name is Hypatia of Alexandria, and she was the victim of one of the most disgusting atrocities in human history.

The story of how Hypatia came to be in Raphael's work is a fascinating one. He was commissioned by the clergy to decorate the rooms of the Apostolic Palace in the Vatican. The fresco took him two years to complete, between 1509 and 1511. Raphael was required to show the patronizing Bishop preliminary sketches of the fresco (a matter of painful frustration for any artist). Raphael had placed Hypatia to the very centre left in the foreground, beneath Plato and

Aristotle, on the marble steps. Upon perusing the sketches, the Bishop asked, "Who is the beautiful lady in the middle?" Raphael replied, "She is Hypatia of Alexandria, the most famous student of the School of Athens. She was a professor of philosophy, mathematics and astronomy at the University of Alexandria and certainly one of the greatest thinkers ever."

The Bishop at once commanded him to remove her.

Hypatia was a Greek woman who lived and worked 1600 years ago in the great beating heart of the intellectual world, the famous Library of Alexandria, in Egypt. Under Roman rule, Alexandria was then part of the Eastern Empire governed from Constantinople, not Rome. The library itself was part of the museum (the Temple of the Muses) and the center of the university. It had been built and patronized by the Ptolemaic dynasty, of which Cleopatra had been the last to rule. It was created in the third Century BCE in the time of Alexander the Great, and was totally destroyed seven centuries later. Its destruction is still a disputed and tragic semi-mystery.

Hypatia was a scientist, physicist, mathematician and astronomer, but her primary role was Head of the Neo-Platonist School of Philosophy. This was a time when women were still considered to be mere property with little or no prospects, yet under the protection and guidance of her devoted father, Theon, the last head of the Museum of Alexandria, Hypatia was able to move freely and confidently about the city, teach science and philosophy to men, debate politics and the finer points of classical literature, whilst arrayed in the dignified robes of a scholar. Surviving accounts stand testimony to her natural beauty.

Socrates Scholasticus, a fifth Century historian wrote of her:

"There was a woman at Alexandria named Hypatia, daughter of the philosopher Theon, who made such attainments in literature and science, as to far surpass all the philosophers of her own time. Having succeeded to the school of Plato and Plotinus, she explained the principles of philosophy to her auditors, many of whom came from a distance to receive her instructions. On account of the self-possession and ease of manner which she had acquired in consequence of the cultivation of her mind, she not infrequently appeared in public in the presence of the magistrates. Neither did she feel abashed in going to an assembly of men. For all men on account of her extraordinary dignity and virtue admired her the more."

Hypatia wasn't just extraordinary because she was a female philosopher, she was known during her time to be the greatest philosopher of Alexandria. She taught Platonic and Aristotelian philosophy, edited her father's work on Euclidean geometry, taught Pythagorean mathematics, and wrote her own works on astronomy and geometry — alas now lost to us. She invented certain scientific instruments: an astrolabe for measuring the positions of the sun, moon and planets, an apparatus for distilling water, and a graduated brass hydrometer for measuring the specific gravity of liquids.

She believed that all boys and girls should be educated and that superstition was the greatest obstacle to true knowledge and learning. She once wrote:

"Fables should be taught as fables, myths as myths, and miracles as poetic fancies. To teach superstitions as truth is one of the most terrible things. The mind of a child accepts them, and only through great pain, perhaps even tragedy can the child be relieved of them."

We have only fragments and small excerpts of Hypatia's teachings, but it is obvious that she was no friend of religion. She wrote:

"No priests should be allowed to force their beliefs on you and rob you of your right to evolve your own way of life."

And:

"All formal dogmatic religions are fallacious and must never be accepted by self-respecting persons as final."

Her father had invested in her as would any father of the time invest in the future of a son. Hypatia's influence and fame eclipsed that of her father, indeed eclipsed the fame of any man of her city. Her bearing was one of a confident and beautiful woman, secure in the ability of her mind and practical abilities. She did not want to marry and rejected many suitors, perhaps fearing that a traditional union would limit her freedom of movement and accomplishment.

During her time, Christianity was evolving strongly into theocratic rule (often violent) and she found herself at the very epicenter of a clash between civilization and barbarism. Barbarism won. She inspired hatred in Cyril the Archbishop, who sought to stamp out any "pagan" influence in politics and culture in Alexandria. This hatred was also the result of her abiding friendship with Cyril's main enemy, Orestes, the Roman Prefect, who often sought Hypatia's counsel in matters of political and philosophical importance.

According to Damascius, the last head of the School of Athens, writing one hundred years after Hypatia's death, this hatred was also borne of some jealousy:

"Hypatia's style was like this: she was not only well-versed in rhetoric and in dialectic, but she was as well wise in practical affairs and motivated by civic-mindedness. Thus she came to be widely and deeply trusted throughout the city, accorded welcome

and addressed with honor. Furthermore, when an archon was elected to office, his first call was to her, just as was also the practice in Athens…Now the following event took place. Cyril the bishop of the opposite sect was passing Hypatia's house and noticed a hubbub at the door, "a confusion of horses and of men," some coming, others going and yet others standing and waiting. He asked what was the meaning of the gathering and why there was a commotion at the house. Then he heard from his attendants that they were there to greet the philosopher Hypatia and that this house was hers. This information gave his heart such a prick that he at once plotted her murder."

In the year 415 AD, as Hypatia continued to lecture, invent and write, she was in her chariot on her way to the university when a fanatical mob of Christians and desert monks, called into the city by Cyril, assaulted her. They stripped her naked and dragged her through the city to a church where she was beaten and then flayed alive with razor-sharp oyster shells until her flesh had been torn from her body. They dismembered her then burned her mutilated corpse for all to see. Her works were burned with the remains of her body. Alexandria succumbed to Christian theocratic rule and the beginning of the Dark Ages ensued. Soon after her death, the Alexandrian library, museum and university were obliterated.

Henceforth the memory of Hypatia, her achievements and teachings were deemed to be an enemy of

Christianity. In reality, she was the last, great, classical philosopher standing between an age of free intellectual inquiry and the looming shadows of dogmatic intellectual slavery. This descending darkness was to bind free thought in a mental prison for another 1300 years, until 18th Century Enlightenment thinking would again light a path to liberty.

No one was ever brought to justice for Hypatia's brutal torture and death, but Cyril the Archbishop was later canonized by the church as a saint.

And so 1100 years later, Renaissance artist Raphael, commanded by a bishop to remove Hypatia from his great School of Athens fresco, committed a wonderful act of bold deception. He moved her from the center to the left, between Pythagoras and Parmenides, he lightened her skin to be many shades more pale than a Greco-Alexandrian woman's skin would have been, and he disguised her features to resemble that of the ruling Pope's most beloved nephew. Thus Hypatia was resurrected in art and stands among history's most exceptional minds in Raphael's timeless work.

When I study her in this extraordinary work of art my heart always sets a little to aching. All the other philosophers are busy studying their works, discussing matters of great importance and buzzing with the energy of instructing some of their students. But Hypatia stands alone in her white martyr's robes, side-on with her solitary gaze on us, the spectators. Her beautiful eyes silently, but assuredly, entreat us not to forget — as history almost did — that she too deserves to be in this venerable gathering of philosophy's greatest men.

THE EMANCIPATION OF WOMEN & SEXUAL FREEDOM

In 1792, during the early days of America's radical experiment in self-governance, an Englishwoman on the other side of the Atlantic Ocean was writing a book. Her name was Mary Wollstonecraft and the book was titled, "A Vindication of the Rights of Woman."

At exactly the time of her writing this important book, the French Revolution was raging. Their famous political document, "A Declaration of the Rights of Man & of the Citizen" had been penned and enacted. King Louis XVI & Marie Antoinette were one year away from being executed by their own citizens. The whole of Europe was watching this infamously messy overthrow of a monarchy by The People.

Wollstonecraft argued that because women were the mothers and early educators of the young, society would be much improved if it were nurtured by women who were well-educated. She argued that the female mind was just as deserving of an education as its male counterpart, and she excoriated men for encouraging excessive emotional sentimentality in women by maintaining their ignorance and expecting very little else from them.

Reason, Wollstonecraft instructed, was the defining attribute of a human being whether male or female. It was what set people apart from just being animals. To be able to weigh judgments objectively led to a better life and a better civilization in which to live that life. She believed that both men and women ought to be held to similar standards of value, those being at their very foundation a commitment to Reason, Virtue & Knowledge. She lay the case down clearly that these standards were the very well-spring of all that was noble about humanity, regardless of which sex one was born.

The middle-class women of Wollstonecraft's time were educated to an extent, but her criticism led her to point out that this education was mostly about how to please men by outwardly appearing to be accomplished and virtuous, rather than actually *being* accomplished and virtuous. She scathingly observed that the lack of intellectual development of the female mind kept women in an ornamental state of arrested-development and shamefully shallow and useless. In this artificially childish mode, how could women even hope to be adequate companions for their men-folk who ruled the world?

Unlike modern feminists, Wollstonecraft never pushed the argument that men and women were equals (outside of a God's eye view) — it was obvious that nature had formed men to be physically stronger than women, and in possession of greater powers of endurance. But she threw down the challenge to men that if they were indeed the superior sex, why not level the educational playing field and prove it? If it were shown to be so, then the worst that could possibly happen was that society would end up with a lot of women who were markedly improved from what they used to be.

The tumultuous times of revolution served to help Wollstonecraft's arguments take hold. The natural rights of men had been the foundation of a political lurch toward democracy. Wollstonecraft's book asserted that women were born with exactly the same *natural rights*.

Although heavily criticized (of course) "Vindication" was a remarkably successful book that was translated into French and printed in England & America. During its first year of sales a second edition was required to meet the demands of Wollstonecraft's many new readers around the Anglo-Saxon world.

Medicine

Along with people like Mary Wollstonecraft, who made the case for women's rights philosophically (politics follows philosophy), the greatest helping hand toward emancipating women came not from the famous Suffragettes, as most people now believe, but from the world of science and medicine.

Before the 20th Century, giving birth to babies was a serious matter of life and death. Puerperal fever, from which Wollstonecraft herself died, and hemorrhaging, were the usual culprits in claiming the life of a new mother, but also general infections from slack sanitary conditions. Germ theory was being investigated slowly during the 19th Century, but had not been scientifically proved in any convincing way as to alter the daily practice of ordinary medicine.

This meant that far too many women died from complications in pregnancy and childbirth, making the mortality rate of females very high. Infants too, suffered and died before their time. They died from diseases which infants in the West seldom die from now: measles, mumps, colds, flu, polio, rheumatic fever, smallpox, chickenpox, bronchitis, tonsillitis, rubella, diphtheria, typhus, typhoid, tetanus, tuberculosis and asthma.

What dramatically changed this picture were

antibiotics, vaccinations, blood transfusions and surgeries. Before we had the benefit of these incomparable gifts of science, in every respect life was a staggeringly fragile thing which could be carried off by so very many threats outside one's control. To be able to bear healthy children and grow them to adulthood was not an expected given for any mother; in fact, statistically, if you were lucky enough to survive the birth of a child in the mid -19th Century (one out of every eight women did not), there was a ten percent chance the child would not live to see its first birthday.

With life on these precarious terms, how many women would actually choose to have a career outside of the home instead of being with her beloved children day-to-day?

The choice of women to become formally educated and to pursue careers, at the same time as raising families, was made possible by the excellence of Western medicine.

Birth Control

To give a woman control over her reproductive system is to give her a large measure of control over her destiny.

Contraception became widely available in the mid 20th

Century. Before that time there had been forms of contraception on the market, but they were not greatly reliable and often caused more trouble than they were worth. It was quality condoms and the oral contraceptive pill which overturned the accepted order of things.

The advent of The Pill released the bulk of women from confining their sex lives to marriage. At first The Pill was only prescribed to married women, but as the right to self-determination in all matters became a solid norm for Western women, an active sex life without the worry of an unwanted pregnancy became every woman's right. Whomever a woman slept with became just a matter of personal preference rather than an action which would call society's harsh judgment down upon her head in any significant way. Those who valued the tradition of sex being confined to marriage carried on living accordingly, and those who did not did likewise.

The effect of this change on society can be debated from a moral standpoint until the proverbial cows come home. Western women claimed their sexual freedom as part of their natural right to a self-determined life.

Technology

The massive leap of technology during the 20th

Century changed everything for the liberated ease of Western women. Household electricity, sewing machines, washing machines, dishwashers, electric ovens, microwave ovens, vacuum cleaners, supermarkets and cars allowed women to knock off their housekeeping and grocery shopping before ten o'clock in the morning. Housekeeping and cooking were no longer an all-day everyday enterprise. In light of the feminist movement, it is a great irony that the very things which helped free women out from under the domestic drudgery of so-called "male oppression" came directly from the hands of male inventors, engineers, producers and businessmen. I'm not sure that women have ever really absorbed this fact.

A Word on Feminism & Misogyny

Feminism and misogyny are two sides of a single coin; both are a gratuitous absorption in resentment of the opposite sex.

Feminists like to argue that their novel philosophy paved the way for the Suffragette movement, which in early 20th Century America gained women equal voting rights in politics. The truth is, during this time the radical idea of male Universal Suffrage (the vote of men outside the business and land-owning class) had already been enacted. Suffragettes rode that political wave along with the goodly ladies of the 100 year-old Temperance movement, and the two major issues of the day — Prohibition and the Female Vote — powerfully joined forces. Prohibition was the first to win in 1914, becoming the US Constitution's Eighteenth Amendment. The resulting legislation, the Volstead Act, prohibited the production, sale, and transport of alcohol in all States.

I can barely think of any institution outside of black slavery which resulted in so much unnecessary damage to American society. Drinking and brewing alcohol was brutally forced underground to the dark dealings of the black-market, which created an unprecedented bubble of crime, poverty, and murder at a time when the US economy needed the free market more than ever to help employ the masses.

The Great Depression became synonymous with Prohibition from 1929 to 1933. Prohibition's huge misstep in American politics was fueled by the emotionalist fires of feminism. American women gained the vote in 1920 (35 years after New Zealand & South Australian women) but they ought to give salute to the misguided Temperance movement a little more, and the hysterical Suffragettes a little less. They will not do this, however, because the social crusade of feminism hitched its wagon firmly to the progressive politics of the Left; any association with the staunchly conservative, Christian-based Temperance ladies of that time does not fit their liberal image.

One of most popular feminists of the last two decades is American Naomi Wolf, author of the bestselling 90s book, *The Beauty Myth*. In her book, she bombards the beauty industry for being the oppressors of Western women through pressuring them to conform to modern ideas of popular beauty portrayed by the media. Men also pressure women to conform to these modern images of beauty, according to Wolf. I have no doubt that this is true — apart from the "oppressors" and "myth" bits. Pressure is not the same scourge as oppression.

It is no myth that human beings greatly value displays of physical beauty. This idea was writ large in ancient Greek art and then recaptured later in the 16th Century Renaissance (the rebirth of ancient Greek art) and has been with us ever since. In all eras of history, some people are gifted by nature to be more beautiful than others. This arresting tendency in human beings to enjoy viewing beauty has its roots in the origins of our species, Darwin's sexual selection. It can hardly be damned if we are to live within the identity of our natures. Western culture has allowed for the open admiration of beauty because it is a human value and a pleasure, rather than some perilous evil. When this is accepted by individuals without any shame, the larger human question becomes: why is something beautiful to me and in what way do I relate to it?

The 20th Century Russian-American philosopher Ayn

Rand, wrote boldly in 1957, *"Show me the woman a man sleeps with and I will tell you his valuation of himself."* In other words: what gets him off is a reflection of his inner version of himself. His self-esteem levels in bedding a woman for his physical need are felt by the type of woman she is, and the intimate comfort zone, or its lack, which she allows him; the actual sexual act cannot physically be faked without being obvious, hence male sensitivity about performance — which, in a healthy male, usually includes her pleasure.

But what sorts of men insist on a tradition that their women don't feel any sexual pleasure because their clitorises & inner labia have been removed? What sorts of men would kill a daughter or wife, or throw acid in her face, for the so-called crime of tempting a random male to view the unveiled hair on her head? To the culture which allows men to dictate such horrible traditions, Naomi Wolf gives a free pass.

Modern feminists consistently do this because when they hooked up their wagon to the politics of the Left, they took up the cause of multiculturalism. Multiculturalism's overriding dogma holds that *all cultures are equal regardless of the diverse practices of each culture* (reads like a barn wall maxim in a dystopian fable).

Multiculturalism has proved to be a much higher value to this movement than the liberation of women, and I wish they could just admit it. Let it be said that they have betrayed every female value they once identified themselves as standing for. In politics, Angela Merkel is now their most egregious figurehead, seconded only by Hillary Rodham Clinton. I deeply wish these women had been trusted only to bake scones, instead of directing world foreign policy.

In the last year, Merkel has facilitated into Europe some one million Muslim immigrants (the real number is estimated to be much higher but is not actually known), with at least another million set to come in 2016. The New Year celebrations in Cologne, Stockholm, and other European cities just "celebrated" with thousands of male, war-torn, superstitious, malcontents let loose on democratic societies full of easy-going, fair Teutonic girls with their abundant cleavages only an eye-line away. Throw into this potent mix the fashionable nihilism of rap music and death metal, drugs, alcohol and general intellectual vacuity — did Angela Merkel not think this through at all? Does she not understand humans?

In the name of tolerant European society, which Merkel's office of Chancellor is supposed to protect, she willingly chose the lie of multiculturalism over the liberated interests of Europe's young women, who may even have agreed with her, though I think will not thank her. Just as feminists (and religionists) erroneously stoked the excessively emotional fires of the Prohibition blunder in the early 20th Century, they are now fueling the Islamic Immigration Crisis with an unchecked sentimental outlook. A gross want of sound objective judgment is a truly frightening trait in any politician who wields real power.

Merkel dramatically opened the floodgates of Europe to *welfare-dependent* Sunni Muslim males between the ages of 18 – 35; soaked-in-Sharia-law misogynists who are sensitive about their wives' and sisters' hair being visible, at exactly the same time that it was reported on every media outlet in the world, that this demographic was the very same one being heavily recruited for the Islamic State's terror tactics in Western nations. The only goal of this network is to commit acts of bloodshed on civilians as an asymmetrical war tactic. Another favored tactic used by this demographic is rape, and in Islamic societies, rape is always the woman's fault.

Western men have accepted that women have an undeniable sexual power over them — that's part of the thrill of being a heterosexual mammal on-the-make. To this they have to be charming, or at least something close to rich or tolerable, in order to be able to *win* sex and affection. But young Middle Eastern men arriving from incomparably barbaric warzones do not exhibit the same basic manners. On

New Year's Eve 2015, European women suddenly found themselves roaming around on Planet of the Apes, in their own cities.

Back in August 30th 2008, while the multinational forces were engaged in battle with the terror army Al Qaeda in Iraq, an article titled "Behind the veil lives a thriving Muslim sexuality" by Naomi Wolf, appeared in the *Sydney Morning Herald*. Ms. Wolf had taken time to travel into Muslim countries to discuss female issues with Muslim women inside their homes. She cited specifically the countries of Jordan, Morocco and Egypt as the places where she did this.

Ms. Wolf wrote, *"...It is not that Islam suppresses sexuality, but that it embodies a strongly developed sense of its appropriate channeling - toward marriage, the bonds that sustain family life, and the attachment that secures a home."*

It doesn't really matter how the West interprets veiling, talk-about-a non-issue (we don't have to do it outside of the antiquated convent), but what you'd think might matter to a Western feminist who deemed this topic important enough to write about while her country was engaged in a war, are the consequences for many Muslim women if they refuse the veil.

In July 2013 Al Arabiya reported that a fifteen-year-old girl named Amira committed suicide by shooting herself with her father's handgun when she was subjected to violence from her family because she would not wear her head scarf. She was Egyptian.

In March 2014 Almadenah news agency in Jordan reported that: *"The Amman Sharia Court of Appeal has accepted a lawyer's objection to a female witness from testifying for not wearing the hijab, which the court said would affect the fairness and honesty in her testimony from 3/2/2014. According to the fatwa, which the court's decision was based on women who aren't covered up are "sluts," and that gives those women a bad name."*

In May 2012, Fox News reported on a Christian woman named Vivian Salameh, who was fired by the Dubai Islamic Bank for not wearing a head scarf. She is Jordanian.

Also in 2012, in the month of March, and on a very related note, sixteen-year-old Amina Filali committed suicide by ingesting rat poison, because by law she was forced to marry the man who had raped her. She was in the habit of wearing a head scarf, and she was Moroccan. (Morocco has since repealed this diabolical law in 2014.)

After Ms. Wolf's kumbaya connection with Muslim women in Jordan, Morocco and Egypt, I wonder if she takes any comfort in the knowledge that such a law may not have been enforced in order to oppress girls like Amina, but rather because Islam *"embodies a strongly developed sense of [sexuality's] appropriate channeling - toward marriage, the bonds that sustain family life, and the attachment that secures a home."*

Amina Filali did not see it that way.

I understand the difference between overt and private sexual attention, and I don't think it is a distinction which is always silly for women to consider, but the best of Muslim men, by the standards of the Koran, don't just have to shun *promiscuous* expressions of sexuality, they are obligated to repress all outward hints of publicly visible female beauty, in order to not be constantly reminded how sexually powerful women are. (Despite his multiple covered wives, Osama Bin Laden's ample porn stash found with him in Abbatobad showed his brethren just how hard this may be to do.)

Have feminists sunk so low that this is the stuff they are now willing to let pass, while they keep pointing an irrelevant finger at the West's fascination with highly visible sexuality?

Yes, they have sunk that low. They have proven to be unconditionally multicultural-conscious rather than liberty-conscious. For shame!

FREEDOM OF SPEECH AND OF THE PRESS

As well as freedom of religion, the First Amendment covers the rights of individuals to speak or write freely about any topic, including criticism of an incumbent government. Free from what, you may ask? From physical force — force initiated by other individuals or by the State.

This is the current Western freedom under the steadiest assault, which is profoundly disconcerting because it is the one on which all other freedoms hang.

For a man who never looked favorably upon the idea of martyrdom, Enlightenment hero Thomas Jefferson wrote these unusual words to his friend, William G. Munford. The context was a discussion on the progress of science, medicine, innovation and culture:

"To preserve the freedom of the human mind & freedom of the press, every spirit should be ready to devote itself to

martyrdom; for as long as we may think as we will, & speak
as we think, the condition of man will proceed in improvement."

The realms of thought and speech precede the realm of physical actions. Jefferson understood this world of ideas to be sacred to man, sacred and literally untouchable.

Ideas are conceptual survival tools which are the result of having a human nature, they are metaphysical, not man-invented. For a government to justly use force, or an individual to justly harm another, there has to be a concrete act committed and a physical victim of that act as incontrovertible evidence. A system of law must not legislate against ideas themselves — it would be the wrong point of intervention in healthy civic affairs.

We know that totalitarian governments in the 20th Century controlled language; from the Nazis' National Socialism to Mao's China and the Soviet Unions' Marxist Communism. All this was unforgettably set to satire in George Orwell's 1945 classic novel "Animal Farm." On the barn wall the farm's written maxim, *"All animals are equal,"* was stealthily amended to read, *"All animals are equal, but some animals are more equal than others."* Orwell's later dystopian novel "1984" describes the government controlled language of totalitarianism as "Newspeak" — the only collection of words and phrases allowed to be spoken by citizens.

As the West now stands, in over 28 democratic countries people can be arrested for "hate speech" — that is (although the legal definitions are hazy and hard to enforce) governments can fine and imprison citizens for verbally hurting someone's feelings. This includes punishing those who demonstrate such a limp grasp on reality that they deny the genocide of the Jews ever happened under the Nazi regime. It can also include punishing a person for making fun of the prophet of Islam by featuring Mohammad in a satirical cartoon, representing blasphemy. When these cases come up, the umbrage-filled prosecutors make a lot of noise about "protecting human dignity."

History has proven that the only way to protect human dignity is for people to be able to insult others as a principle of the freedom of speech, and have a skin thick enough to take the backlash. But if the backlash is violent retaliation enacted physically (bodily harm or theft of property) then the law traditionally comes down hard against the physical abuser, not the verbal one, for by any standard of objectivity there is a victim in this case. That is the correct point of intervention by the law if the goal is to have a thriving live-and-let-live culture. The Social Justice Warrior code that one has a *right* not to have one's feelings offended is as subjective as it is weak-spirited. European Jewry did not suffer because the

Nazis spoke out and wrote against them (if only!). They suffered because they were laid-off, robbed, terrorized and murdered — without recourse to the law, because the laws had all been radically amended to exclude them.

Jews were considered the "less-than-equal animals," yet they rose to every form of professional expertise, from music to law to medicine. They certainly did not make an impression on their host societies by committing acts of terrorism on civilian life.

Yet it is currently fashionable (and much less than insightful) to compare the old European Jewish Question with the modern Muslim Immigration Crisis — as if they are in any way comparable. You will see this comparison consistently in media articles and video clips which usually include in their titles some blend of the words: Islamophobia, Anti-Semitism & Hate Speech.

Just to put this false comparison to bed, in pre-1939, the Jewish Diaspora were productive members of society who earned a name for themselves by being competent, family-oriented, tough, sharp-minded and hardworking in every field of professional expertise they ever touched. They were also the most persecuted race of people ever known through every epoch in which they existed, dating back to the fall of Jerusalem to the Romans in 70 AD. Hitler did not have them exterminated because they were a lagging problem, he did so because they were a mystifying success, and he happened to be a psychopathic misfit (who failed to gain acceptance into any art school or architectural academy in Vienna). He implemented the politics of envy writ large for the whole world to see, and have to nauseatingly clean up after.

The question of today's news media reporting with uneasiness on mass Islamic immigration into Western countries has its basis in the fact that their plenteous homelands are a tyrannical, murderous, sectarian mess (even worse before the Oil Age), and that murder has made itself concretely felt on European and American soil with alarming frequency, before and since 9/11/2001.

It is compounded by the fact that often when people commit acts of free speech in the West by drawing attention to this savagery in print or film, such as Theo Van Gogh, The Danish Jyllands-Posten Mohammad Cartoons, Charlie Hebdo, or the American Defence Initiative's Draw Mohammad Contest, an overwhelming amount of Muslims (backed by multiculturally-obsessed Westerners) think that the proper response to this is brutal violence because Muslims are offended. By law in a properly free society, their hurt feelings should count for absolutely nothing as it shouldn't count for offended Jews, Christians, Buddhists, Hindus or Baha'is.

Westerners have had to fight tooth-and-claw with each other to forge governing parliaments, where demoralizing and demolishing one's enemies by one's wits in debate is an important part of the democratic digestion of ideas. (If anyone doubts this, just observe the current 2016 American Presidential debates, which, at times a cringe-worthy spectacle, are exactly as they have to be in order to extract the one willing person in a population of 320 million, whom a majority of citizens think is the right one to steer them through the labyrinth of their times.) This blistering process happens to stop *the vast majority of ideological conflicts* from spilling over into physical violence. It is not a stage that can be skipped. The Islamic nations have not yet succeeded in valuing this battle of ideas, even with the example of the West looming large in front of their beards and burkas. So, like Hitler, far too many of them, seek to physically destroy the people who serve as a living reproach to their medieval ideology. Their 7th Century Holy Book gives them permission to kill anybody representing this reproach - infidels; also known as *us*. To the extent that they believe their Koran to be "truth" we are in physical danger.

If Muslims really believe that the ways of their Prophet are the answer to all of man's complex problems, they can prove it by showing how successful they and their civilizations actually are. They cannot do this though, because it flies in the face of an extremely objective judge — reality.

The other glaring difference between these false press narratives that Islamophobia somehow compares with pre- 1939 Anti-Semitism is that the European Jews were persecuted as a *race* through precise documentation of their ancestry. Islam is not a race, it's a political ideology with a smattering of religion — a theocracy. Muslims are from many countries. Their binding value, not withstanding their warring sects, is an ideology of a revived world Caliphate and an afterlife, as promised in the Koran. Jews, unlike Christians and Muslims, do not believe in an afterlife — it may be one of the reasons why so many of them have a remarkable tendency to make this life count for something exceptional by way of human endeavor.

When any culture provides a robust arena for the fierce competition of ideas to be expressed without hurt feelings derailing the issue, the men and women of such a civilization can only improve, not devolve. When human discourse is openly inclined toward the transparent instead of the repressed, the best ideas have a chance to win out because they can be openly fought for. That fight is the crucible of all civilized innovation from ancient Athenian philosophy to NASA.

A COMMITMENT TO
SCIENTIFIC INQUIRY

Like trees and graceful giraffes, ancient mountains and stars, human beings have been forged from purely natural phenomena. The singular goal of all scientific thought is to understand how natural phenomena work.

In 350 BCE, it was Aristotle of Athens, who, in contradiction to his formidable teacher Plato, asserted that the workings of the Universe were intelligible to the human mind through observation and experience. This, along with Aristotle's formulations of logic, created the scientific empirical method. More evocative of pagan thinking, Plato taught that every physical object we see has its real *identity* in another dimension — the realm of Forms — so that when we recognize with our sense of sight an object, say "a horse," it is because there is an idea of "horse" which exists already in the realm of forms and concepts.

Aristotle taught the very opposite: we recognize with

our sense of sight a thing called "a horse" because horses exist in the material world and we have seen them before, therefore we remember them from experience. The identity of every "thing" and "concept" has its reference point in physical reality, not in some immaterial other-world. (Occam's Razor springs to mind.)

It is very easy to understate the impact of Aristotle's opposing view, so I'll say it this way: it was the difference between a worldview which could lead to unlocking the hidden secrets of nature, and a worldview which could only ever allow for being mystified by them. It is in this very real sense that one can say of Plato that he was the father of all mysticism, and of Aristotle that he was the father of all science.

In light of this, it is an awful irony that it was Aristotle whom the medieval Catholic Church dogmatized a thousand years later. They claimed him as their philosopher because his early Greek view of the sun, moon and planets orbiting around Earth reinforced their mystic mindset that Earth and Man were the very pinnacles of God's creation, and God represented Aristotle's idea of an Unmoved Mover - the source of all life. The malevolent Inquisition used the innocent error of Aristotle's antiquated cosmology to bludgeon Galileo, when his own observations and calculations pointed toward the truth of a heliocentric view. (I'm reminded of the late Christopher Hitchens' book title, "*God is Not Great: How Religion Poisons Everything.*")

Still, it wasn't all terrible in the end. Through the late Middle Age period, the Catholic Church kept Aristotle's surviving works alive (in spite of being the persecutors of all non-Christian philosophy), after they passed back into Europe from the custodial hands of the Islamic philosophers.

Influenced heavily by the Islamic Golden Age philosophers -Al Farabi (872 AD) and Avicenna (980 AD), Arab philosopher Averroes (1126 AD) made a monumental impact on both worlds with his commentaries on Aristotle and Plato. Averroes taught the Deist view that natural phenomena followed natural laws, originally created by Allah but left to do their own thing. He came up against the theologians of his religion who asserted the Theist view that no natural phenomenon happens without the divine will of Allah dictating its every step — the epitome of an interventionist God. (Jews and Christians believed this too, only their Allah was Jehovah.) Islamic theologians steadily crushed scientific thinking, condemning Greek philosophy to be "un-Islamic," which is the primary reason their cultures never produced a Renaissance or Enlightenment.

In the West, the potent embryo of Aristotelian

thought became embedded in Scholasticism, enabling it to burst out unbounded after the Protestant Reformation of the 16th Century ended theocratic rule.

Although fundamentally a Theist rather than a Deist, Thomas Aquinas (1225 AD) would become Europe's answer to Averroes — a Roman Catholic monk who burned bright for the teachings of Plato and Aristotle but had to interpret them through the ultimate lens of religion. Aquinas was the main founder of the Scholastic formal education system of the Catholics, which emphasized Aristotle's applications of logic and syllogism. He got this from Averroes. When Aquinas wrote his own works about Aristotle with his known source as Averroes, he referred to the former as just "the Philosopher" and the latter as "the Commentator." At the risk of overstating the case of Averroes' influence on Europe, there are many historians who refer to Thomas Aquinas as an Averroeist, even though it was against Averroes that he wrote some of his strongest disputations; it only shows the wide-reaching importance of Averroes at the time. Aquinas and Scholasticism became the intellectual spine of Catholic Orthodoxy in order to try to synthesize Greek logic with Christian theology. This is how the Inquisition 340 years later came to beat poor Galileo about the head with Aristotelian refutations on cosmology, as if he were accusing God himself — and in truth, Aristotle was a god of such philosophic magnitude, his works on ethics, reason, metaphysics and logic carry a natural and deserved authority. Any serious thinker wanted him on their side. He just happened to be wrong about cosmological revolutions, as every ancient Greek was, but even these were not to be fully proven wrong for 1300 years, by Newton (1672).

Medieval cosmology was proven wrong because of two world-changing innovations: the telescope and mathematical calculus. The telescope enabled men to see closer into planetary movements, calculus enabled them to measure small changes over vast distances with great accuracy. Newton was highly proficient with both. If Newton could have reached back in time to show Aristotle his scientific findings, acquired by the power of Aristotle's observant logic, Aristotle would have wept a river of pure egoistic joy not only for the elegant grandeur of the real cosmos, but also for man; for his understanding the significance of his need to know in the face of cosmic insignificance.

When Newton wrote the rather modest words about himself in a letter to his great rival Robert Hooke:

"If I have seen further it is by standing on the shoulders of Giants."

I'd wager my best diamonds that not only did he have in mind Copernicus, Galileo and Kepler — he was saluting Aristotle, the teacher of scientific inquiry to them all.

The Telescope & Beyond

The telescope for terrestrial purposes was already in use in Europe at the time of Galileo, who then made his own and aimed it into the night skies of Renaissance Italy. By the time Newton invented his much superior reflecting telescope, he and Gottfried Leibnitz had also gifted the world with the ability to apply mathematics to infinitesimal movements — calculus. Armed with these two innovations, Newton finally set the whole world straight on just how the solar system moved. He also described the workings of the force of universal gravity although he did not know what gravity actually was, as we do not today.

Because the telescope had so successfully enhanced one of our major senses — that of sight, the furthering of science after Newton became a matter of inventing instruments to push the boundaries of human sense-perception for greater powers of observation. On the basis of Newtonian physics, those of us living today have all seen the stunning beauty of other-galaxy nebulae photographed deep in our universe and beamed back to Earth by that technological prize, the Hubble telescope. But science took a great leap forward not just because of man's inclination to gaze into the stars, but also to see down into the hidden structures of all matter.

The microscope was widely used in the 17th Century. Robert Hooke, an English natural philosopher published his book Micrographia in 1665. Micrographia contained up close drawings of life seen under a microscope — fleas, lice, plants, insects, the eyes of flies. It is Hooke who coined the term "cell" after observing the structure of leaves. After his contemporary, Antonie van Leeuwenhoek in Holland, developed a microscope powerful enough to magnify objects at 300 times their natural size, germs causing diseases were able to be observed.

Girolamo Fracastoro of Italy, physician of the Council of Trent, published a book as early as 1546 on contagious diseases where he wrote that tiny "spores" were the transmitters of infection and could be passed through the environment without physical contact between people. What Fracastoro did not have were any scientific instruments to prove his theory, which we now know was on track with reality. He is remembered rightly as the first father of Germ Theory. It would take until the 19th Century for his theory to actually be proved by John Snow (1854) who showed that cholera was spread to people through contaminated water, Louis Pasteur (1864) whose formal experiments yielded the dire connection between unsanitary doctors' hands and puerperal fever in new mothers, and Robert Koch (1880) whose research in microbiology and pathogens formed the scientific base of Germ Theory. Gone were the days where disease was considered to be punishment by God for sins (except in some quarters this was still put forth as feasible in cases of syphilis for obvious reasons, just as the God-Hates-Fags crowd today are fond of proposing about HIV).

During this time, natural philosopher Charles Darwin published his myth-shattering book on natural selection, The Origin of Species (1859), describing how all forms of life evolved slowly over millions of years, naturally adapting to the environment in a perpetual struggle for survival. This insightful observation about nature revolutionized biology, and, after it was clearly put into words, was considered to be so illuminating that Darwin's contemporary, biologist Thomas Henry Huxley, exclaimed upon reading it, "How extremely stupid not to have thought of that!" Once understood, natural selection seems as obvious as the nose on a Fifth Ape's face. The 20th & 21st Century scientific project of unraveling the human DNA code has proved without doubt that both we and primates have hailed from a common ancestor. Human DNA and Chimpanzee DNA are 98.8 percent identical. All the obvious conceptual differences between humans and chimps are but a 1.2 percent of separation. Darwinism succeeded in being proved beyond anybody's wildest dreams. But Darwin knew that nature was nothing if not brutal. The predatory behavior of animal habits shows this. Natural selection seems so utterly indiscriminate — out of all the species ever to have existed on this planet, nature has eliminated 99 percent of them. The species that have survived have been the ones whose ancestors were able to successfully adapt and live long enough to pass their genes on to the next generation, and so on. Most forms of life have been eliminated along the way: the weak, the defective, the sick, and the forceless; in the natural world they simply didn't make it through time.

Homo sapiens naturally evolved to do something entirely unusual. It's a superb achievement for which only nature can take any credit - we evolved to be able to *invent* the means to take care of our needs. No other known life form does this and it is why Aristotle named us the "rational animal." Take away our rationality and we are nothing but an ape (think ISIS, although that might be a terrible injustice to apes). With our slowly evolving rational capacity we adapted ourselves and evolved our species by being creative — and that is the essence of what we call human.

With this creativity, the story of civilization has been one of man's quests to command the raw forces which have formed him. Natural selection has become man-directed selection where doctors, scientists, entrepreneurs, innovators, teachers, churches, charities and societies make huge efforts to make sure that the weak, the defective, the sick and the forceless are taken care of through acts driven by human empathy, and ideas about morality. Cooperation between individuals in the early days of our species made survival more likely if we lived in tribes rather than in isolation, and so we attached a profound and tangible value to caring about each other. Without acting on feelings of empathy our species would not have survived. The deep-seated human innovation of morality is inextricably bound to our rationality and empathy, or lack of them. These are the attributes Homo sapiens developed which eventually led their resultantly enlarged brains to think in terms of "a world view."

All the world's religions, pagan and monotheistic, were created by the inventive minds of men who did not understand what we know to be science. Man has done this because humans need a world view in order to possess an understanding of their own context as beings-who-contemplate (the rational animal) in a raw but magnificent world. A world view, and your own place within it, expands the ideas which give rise to a moral code, and like everything else, they evolve and adapt over time, having the energy to shape lives far beyond one human lifespan.

Darwinism may be the way nature has formed us, but constructing our civilizations according to the predatory forces of nature does not allow us to flourish, but then neither does denying them. With our ability to contemplate in the forefront of our brains, the force that allows human civilization to flourish, not just to survive, lies in the potential of man to view nature (including oneself) objectively, summarized so well by English philosopher Francis Bacon (1561) as: "Nature to be commanded must be obeyed." It almost goes without saying that to be obeyed nature must first be observed. What philosophical elegance then, defines man's transient agency in his creative ascent toward his own evolution? I can let William Shakespeare answer from *The Tempest*:

"And like the baseless fabric of this vision, The cloud-capped towers, the gorgeous palaces, The solemn temples, the great globe itself—Yea, all which it inherit—shall dissolve, And like this insubstantial pageant faded, Leave not a rack behind. We are such stuff as dreams are made on, and our little life is rounded with a sleep."

The stuff to be a temporal, organic part of the grandeur of nature itself with the powers to observe, to obey and to command *is* the very stuff that dreams are made on — and sadly nightmares too.

CAPITALISM AND INNOVATION

As the singular goal of science is to understand the workings of natural phenomena, the singular goal of innovation is to make these understandings useful. The open trade of new innovation is the very heart of the capitalist economic system. The greatest economic resource which has always been the driver of innovation is the power of the human mind.

We live in a time when the term Capitalist is associated with being a Selfish Pig, or at the very best, an Imperial Bastard (even though imperialism was built on the system of mercantilism, not capitalism). The term is used so pejoratively that it is now obvious most people do not understand what it means, nor recognize capitalism's place in lifting the masses out of poverty.

To get back to basic definitions — capitalism is a socio-economic system which allows capital, that is, monetary profits from the production of goods, to remain in the hands of private citizens to benefit society on a voluntary basis of where one chooses to spend one's money. Communism allows only for the means of production, and resulting profits, to be in the hands of the state then distributed out to the people as the government sees fit; it is the close relation of socialism. Socialism allows for the means of production to remain in the hands of private citizens, but government enforces the right to take profits in the form of high taxations, levies, duties, licenses and tariffs, and to redistribute money out to the infrastructure which private citizens might use (schools, hospitals, roads, welfare and everything else government deems important).

People do not seem to understand that a socio-economic system is itself a moral issue. I say moral, because it is either rationally in accordance with the nature of human beings, or against it. Morality is a tool toward good ends, not an achievement in itself. It is a defining attribute of human beings to want to create and be productive, but to labor for one's own self-betterment is a completely different motivational impetus than having to labor for the betterment of strangers. That is the difference between capitalism and socialism or capitalism and communism. It is also the difference between capitalism and slavery.

The meteoric rise of capitalism in the West happened during the 19th Century. If we were take a bird's eye view of the world before this time, we would be able to see quite clearly that poverty was the normal state of human existence right around the globe, unless one was lucky enough to be born into inherited riches. This meant that the rate of education for the masses was extremely low since children were required to be in the fields working in order to help the family survive. Education was a supreme luxury unavailable to most people.

The birth of capitalism changed this picture completely and was helped on its way by an important book, *The Wealth of Nations*, by Scottish philosopher Adam Smith (1776). Smith laid out the case that the most efficient economy was one where a free market drives trade with little interference from government, and if left alone, the market regulates itself through supply and demand on the basis of robust competition. This is referred to as "the invisible hand" directing the market. The Wealth of Nations highlights three imperative aspects of successful capitalism: division of labor, productivity and a free market. During Smith's time, imperialism ruled the world and controlled their economies through a highly regulated mercantile system.

Mercantilism "protected" economies by encouraging national exports and limiting national imports via high tariffs, tax duties and strict regulations. It was against this system that America's Founding Fathers railed after the British parliament issued the Molasses Act, the Sugar Act, the Stamp Act and the Tea Act — all designed to limit the ability of the American Colonists to compete in an open market. The rum industry within America relied heavily on importing molasses from plantations in the French West Indies, but England, in order to protect plantation owners in their own colonies of the British West Indies, imposed heavy tax duties on imports from non-British islands, which, if paid, would have wiped out the entire industry. American colonists refused to pay and instead relied on smuggling to acquire their precious molasses. After this Act was repealed, the British parliament issued another, the Sugar Act, which halved the actual tax duties required, but England promised extra tenacity from bureaucrats to make sure the tax was enforced and smuggling was punished. These Acts culminated with the infamous Tea Act, which American colonists responded to by dumping three ship-loads of tea into the Boston Harbor — the Boston Tea Party. It was largely these restrictive Acts on open trade which led the Thirteen Colonies to declare their independence from Great Britain and fight the Revolutionary war. They considered these Acts to be a political affront to a very specific kind of freedom — that of the quality of their own livelihoods. Capitalism and free enterprise were the solution.

After the American Revolution was soundly won,

capitalism became especially predominant in the Northern States. The cotton growing industry, heavily focused in the Southern States, exported their goods to England, France and the Northern States for manufacture, their labor force consisting of black slaves. This is why by the time Abraham Lincoln was elected president (1860), the South clung to slavery like men clinging to a barrel in a broiling sea; they were clinging to their threatened economy. In truth the South didn't just cling to slavery, they were fighting like demons to extend it in to the new states and also the Caribbean Islands and Latin America. As new states emerged after 1800, Ohio, Indiana, Kansas, Missouri, Maine — the big question of the time was will they be Slave States or Free States? Plantation owners needed ever more land; cultivating cotton, tobacco and sugar was not only greedy for fresh slaves, it was greedy for fresh soil. Lincoln denied them new lands. The South knew this to be their death knell. Rather than innovate on the industrialized model offered by the North's burgeoning example, they instead fought to secede from the Union. The newly formed Republican party of 1860 was the party of anti-slavery and pro-capitalism (given her admirable success, I do wish Oprah Winfrey could remember this).

The North won the Civil War because it was powered by industry. The Union army's soldiers were better attended to thanks to ever extending railways bringing food, ammunition and medicine to the troops. New European immigrants, proud to now call themselves industrious Americans, gravitated to the bustling cities experiencing high growth because of factories and construction offering employment: Chicago, Detroit, Cincinnati, and Cleveland. In the North only 40 percent of the population lived in agrarian areas, as opposed to 84 percent in the South. Northern farms had been mechanized with threshing machines and mechanical reapers, releasing farmers from the need to employ large groups of laborers, an important factor as to why the North had far more men able to fight a war at the same time as keeping their farms fully operational back home. Innovation and manpower enabled the North to sustain a war economy while the feudal South crumbled into poverty.

In the spring of 1863, Lincoln issued the Emancipation Proclamation and 180,000 blacks went on to serve in the Union army on paid wages, to fight the very men who had enslaved them for centuries — it is little wonder they earned a reputation for being overwhelmingly fierce in the face of battle.

In 1964 at the height of the Cold War, Ronald Reagan spoke these words in his "A Time for Choosing" speech when he endorsed Barry Goldwater for president:

"We're at war with the most dangerous enemy that has ever faced mankind in his long climb from the swamp to the stars, and it's been said if we lose that war, and in so doing lose this way of freedom of ours, history will record with the greatest astonishment that those who had the most to lose did the least to prevent its happening."

Reagan had in mind an enemy not dissimilar to the one we face today, though now it's even more entrenched. No, I'm not referring to Islamofascism (though if the cap fits), I'm referring to the war of social systems; Capitalism versus Everything Else.

During the 20th Century, the story of capitalism in the free world lies in direct contrast to the Bolshevik Revolution of Russia, which brought communism into power for the following eight decades. Communism flatly rejected individual rights as a moral concept, and the Soviet Union nationalized all private business and all private capital, plummeting the totality of its citizenry into homogenized poverty. Collectivism was its binding code, subjugating the individual to the group (euphemistically called "the common good") which meant that any individual had to sacrifice personal advantage and personal freedom to the State — upon the pain of death or the gulag. A totalitarian, miserable, human poverty-pen was the result. (This is presidential hopeful Bernie Sander's current vision for America.)

Meanwhile back in the free world, new phenomena began to emerge: the businessman, the businesswoman and the well-heeled middleclass. This in turn, and by default, helped those still on the breadline. Instead of a lowly laundress having one client who paid her 25 cents per day for a family's washing to be cleaned and ironed, she now had multiple clients looking for her services resulting in a jump to earning $1.50 per day. This was the difference between her putting bread on the family dinner table, or beef. It was also the difference between her being able to keep her children in school or not. These were not small differences, neither were they rare.

If we are to keep this "way of freedom of ours" we must be able to defend its case against those who curse it so self-confidently. Fortunately, it's not that hard to do considering capitalism's benefits, though not perfect, are obvious, but it seems to have accepted a guilty conscience along the way for being far too successful.

The Spirit of Innovation

From the invention of the printing press through to the steam engine, the internal combustion engine, antibiotics, vaccinations, the ability to fly and the Internet, capitalism has driven the free market to double the human lifespan from 40 years (preindustrial revolution) to 78 years (current average life expectancy). It has even put men on another celestial body we call the moon. Now we have private companies such as SpaceX™ and Virgin Galactic™ on a competitive trajectory to blast ordinary citizens up in to space in order to enjoy not only the incomparable view, but the exotic pleasure of free floating in zero gravity. The next great frontier of space exploration is manned missions to Mars.

Communist China could never have conceived these inventions, nor could North Korea, theocratic Iran, Assad's Syria, Saddam Hussein's Iraq nor Saudi Arabia, why? Because the stifling chains on human ingenuity that they bind their citizens in through enforced obedience to their regimes, kill the spirit of innovation at its very conceptual level; human creativity. Humans do not originate innovation without the freedom to enjoy their creations.

The stunting of *homegrown* technological innovation has been the story of the Middle East in the modern context, except Israel. Who was the Henry Ford of the Middle East? Who was their Isaac Newton, Nikola Tesla or Albert Einstein? Who was their Steve Jobs, or is their Elon Musk? Only the capitalist system can truly claim the spirit of innovation as its natural heir. The high standard of living in the West of both personal wealth and individual freedom is all the evidence anyone needs to know this. The spirit of innovation thrives in the context of personal freedom – and capitalism is the only system which respects the natural rights of people to life, liberty and the pursuit of happiness.

~~~

No person of sense, and certainly not I, would claim the West to be perfect, and it never has been. Some of its worst problems have been created directly from within: from wolfish imperialism and self-absorbed narcissism, to the current disgrace of anti-conceptual modern "art," modern "music," empty consumerism and oversexed baseness. Yet it is increasingly clear that its most threatening dilemma is one of historical ignorance toward its own superiority and the lack of passionate valuing which egalitarian Westerners refuse to engage in. They often prefer to politely smile or shrug, then offer some worn-out platitude about "not judging" (this is how we end up with such terrible art — people value mindless self-expression over quality of content). This is nothing more than a polished form of plastic nihilism to keep the huge responsibility of evaluative thinking on the shoulders of the Few and not the Self. This intellectual indifference flies in the face of Thomas Jefferson's cautionary word that: "*Freedom is not the absence of rigor; it is the absence of restraints imposed by others.*" A system created on the benevolent foundation of individual rights and personal liberty will, in the long term, not be able to sustain this evasion, especially with enemies in the world working passionately for no other purpose than the ignoble glory of bringing the West to its knees. This is arguably what happened to ancient Rome.

WORKS CITED

Letters on the English, Voltaire

Declaration of Independence, Thomas Jefferson et al.

Constitution of the United States, various authors

Historia Ecclesiastica, Socrates of Constantinople

Life of Isidore, Damascius

Vindication of the Rights of Woman, Mary Wollstonecraft

Declaration of the Rights of Man & of The Citizen, various authors

The Beauty Myth, Naomi Wolf

Atlas Shrugged, Ayn Rand

"Behind the veil lives a thriving Muslim sexuality," Naomi Wolf, *Sydney Morning Herald*, August 30, 2008

Letter to William Munford by Thomas Jefferson

Animal Farm, George Orwell

God is not Great, Christopher Hitchens

Micrographia, Robert Hooke

On Contagion and Contagious Disease, Girolamo Fracastoro

The Tempest, William Shakespeare

The Wealth of Nations, Adam Smith

ABOUT THE AUTHOR

Olivia Pierson is also the author of "To Love Wisdom – Gateway to the Heroic for the Young" — an introduction to philosophy for young people aged ten to thirteen. She writes about politics, history and culture on her website www.oliviapierson.org.

CPSIA information can be obtained at www.ICGtesting.com
Printed in the USA
LVOW10s1800170816

500540LV00013B/4/P